All Scripture references taken from the KJV of the Holy Bible unless otherwise indicated.

<u>Upgrade: How to Get Out of Survival Mode</u>

Book 1 of The Upgrade Series

by Dr. Marlene Miles

Freshwater Press USA

ISBN: 978-1-960150-31-8

Paperback Version

Copyright 2023 by Dr. Marlene Miles

All rights reserved. No part of this book may be reproduced, distributed or transmitted by any means or in any means including photocopying, recording or other electronic or mechanical methods without prior written permission of the publisher except in the case of brief publications or critical reviews.

## Table of Contents

**Everyone Wants an Upgrade** .................................... 4
**Vacation Days** ............................................................ 6
**Emergency Prayers** ................................................. 11
**Our Provider** ............................................................ 13
**Upgrade Your Life** ................................................... 16
**Five Senses** .............................................................. 18
**Your Prayers** ............................................................ 22
**Vision** ....................................................................... 25
**Survival Mode is for Babies** ................................... 32
**Looking Out** ............................................................. 36
Do What God Does .................................................... 39
What Do We Pray? ..................................................... 41
**Is It Real?** ................................................................. 46
**Real Survival Mode** ................................................. 49
**What Stress Feels Like** ............................................ 53
**Flesh Mode** .............................................................. 62
**Get Out of It** ............................................................. 66
**A Test Deposit** ......................................................... 74
**Chill Out** ................................................................... 76
**Are You Being Manipulated?** .................................. 84
**Christian books by this author:** ............................. 89

# UPGRADE
## How To Get Out Of Survival Mode

Freshwater Press, USA

# Everyone Wants an Upgrade

When I told my family I was looking for an upgrade, they cracked up laughing at me. They didn't believe I was serious, but I was. The previous year, I had upgraded my coffee, so now I was in the market for a full life's upgrade. That's how the books in this series came to be. No matter what you do in the natural, if you spend enough time on it, you'll end up looking in the spiritual realm, at what's really happening and why it's happening in the natural. I ended up looking at my spiritual condition so I could get that upgrade that I wanted in the natural.

Everybody's looking for an upgrade; we want first class seats on a plane, we want premium subscriptions and the best that life can offer. But sometimes we may find that we are in the opposite position of what we really want and what God has planned for our lives.

I believe this book will challenge a serious reset to your life if you give it your attention all the way through.

## Vacation Days

When it comes to your job you don't just tell your boss today that you want tomorrow and the next two weeks off because you're going on vacation. Appalling as this is, some young people believe this is how you conduct yourself in the business world. Perhaps they think if they spring their clandestine plans on you at the last minute, you'll just say, okay. No, that's immature, tacky, unprofessional and will get you fired. You don't call your job in the morning on your way to the airport to get a flight to Cancun to let them know you're going on vacation now. No, you *put in* for that vacation time off six months in advance, sometimes even longer out.

If you go to a big city during a very busy time of the year, such as New Year's Eve, you may need to make hotel reservations well in advance if you expect to stay at that hotel.

We make plans all the time. We make dinner reservations. We buy tickets to future events. We plan ahead all the time. So when it comes to spiritual matters, when it comes to God, why don't we think that God needs any notice? Why do we think that God doesn't need to hear from us? Or that God is just standing around waiting for our whims and wishes to be made known to Him so He can just ZAP things all day and all night at our command? Why do we think that God doesn't need advance *notice*?

You know you want certain things in your life. So do I. Sometimes you want things in your life *tomorrow*. Do you think it's a good idea to just be asking God about it *today*? You give more respect to your job than that. This is God we're talking about. So maybe you want or need things for your life next week. When do you think you should ask God for that?

When do you think you should ask God about that thing, or those things?

When you're having a child, you plan their room. You plan for their schooling. At some point you plan to save for their college or their future, their wedding, or whatever you plan to give them as a gift when they get married. When do you start planning for those events?

When do you start planning for your own retirement? The *day* before you retire? The *week* before you retire? The *month* before you retire? Of course not.

We say we love God. If we say we love someone, how can we also take that person for granted? For example, you're on the way home to see your mom. You call her and tell her, *"Mom I want mac and cheese."* You get home and Mom has made mac and cheese because she's your mom. But you say you love her; you love your mom--, well, her making mac and cheese for you was more of an act of *her* loving you, than you loving her.

We say we love God. Jesus *first* loved us. Then are we to love Him back? Yes, we are. He *first* loved us, the Bible doesn't say He *only* loved us. You are to love the Lord your God with all your heart, with all your soul, and with all your mind, (Matthew 22:37).

We say we love God; we can't take Him for granted by only asking Him for things all the time. Especially we shouldn't be asking God tonight for things that we need tomorrow morning at 7:30 AM.

We can't just show up in in God's face only when we want something from Him. Some of us haven't even ventured into a church since COVID--, that's somewhat understandable, but are we breadcrumbing God, giving Him just a little here and there just to kind of keep Him on the line?

Are we *using* God and giving nothing back? Where is God's praise and His worship? Are we always taking and taking and asking and taking but offering nothing in return-- just our wonderful selves?

When we are asking God for things, what are we asking him for things *for*? For what purpose? James 4:3 says that sometimes we ask God for things, but we don't get those things because we ask with the wrong motives. Asking for things to use for our own pleasures is a wrong motive.

So, in the drama of asking tonight for tomorrow or asking for the mac and cheese while you're on the way home to your mother neither are the best motives and they are both rather near-sighted.

Do you think God likes drama? Do you think God likes being asked tonight for something that might be critically important to you tomorrow? You tell me.

Jesus is the Prince of Peace. Do you think the Prince of Peace likes *drama*? Of course not. So could this be why your life doesn't seem to be going well? Is this why you need an upgrade? Everybody wants an upgrade.

# Emergency Prayers

Here's more drama; the emergency prayer. Do you only pray when you're in a crisis? Do you only pray when you need or want something? Do you only pray prayers of petition asking God for *stuff*? Do you wait until its urgent, things are dire, before you choose to pray? Do you wait until things are a matter of life and death, or survival?

Sometimes you need to pray to set things in agreement with God and Heaven. Sometimes agreement takes time—more time than overnight, or the next day or in a couple of hours.

God is not limited. God can move miraculously. But does He have to move miraculously in your life *all the time*?

God always moves divinely. That's true. But sometimes God will move through other people. And even though God is miraculous, sometimes He may not get your neighbor or your coworker or your friend or your family member to move in enough time to *cause* the thing that you're asking for tonight to happen in the morning.

## Our Provider

I am not saying don't ask God for things because He is our Provider. Yes, we can cry out to God emotionally when we need to. That's very acceptable, but we also cannot get into the flesh, because if we do, our prayers may not make it out of the room that we're in.

God says He'll make the skies bronze, that is if we sin, (Deuteronomy 28:23). That means our prayers seem as though they're going up but then, they might hit the ceiling, or hit the sky of bronze and crash back down to Earth.

Then you might be thinking, well, I thought that Jesus taught us to pray, Give us this day Our Daily Bread. Yes, Jesus did teach that in the Lord's Prayer. But which day? *This* day? It means you pray **each day**, but it doesn't necessarily mean that you only pray for today and only **about** today.

Matthew 6:34 says, *Give no thought of tomorrow.* This is Jesus' preaching the Sermon on the Mount. Jesus then answered by saying, *For the morrow shall take thought of the things of itself so efficient, for the day is its own trouble.*

In other words, today has enough problems to be concerned with without worrying about tomorrow, you see that word, *worry* there. If we look further, look deeper, it says do not be anxious for anything, do not be anxious for the things that God is already taking care of. You in those matters. The fact that there are or will be troubles tomorrow means we should stay prayerful.

The verse doesn't mean don't give a thought to tomorrow. It doesn't mean don't do anything. It means that we don't ***worry*** about it because God's got it. Well, God's got it if we also brought to His attention and we also came into *agreement* with God to make Earth and

Heaven, Heaven and Earth agree so God can move on your behalf, and God could make those things that you need a reality in the Earth.

We have faith, and we believe that tomorrow will come--, even though it's not promised to anyone. You still move in faith, because without faith it is impossible to please God.

# Upgrade Your Life

When God is pleased, we have strength, because the joy of the Lord is our strength. So here's where I tell you how to **upgrade** your life: **Upgrade your prayer life**.

Use some of that planning that you do for your natural life to put into prayer and ask God the things that you are believing for, for your future.

We can take that a bit further. God transcends all time and space, so we can be more like God. We can pray from the place where God says that we are already. If God says we're healed, then we pray from the place of healing, thanking God already for the healing that we have, because we are already speaking from our future like God is. God is far ahead of us. He's already in our tomorrow and tomorrows, so we speak from that place, and we thank God for it.

So now we are praying from God's NOW instead of our now.

Recommended book: <u>Living for the NOW of God</u>, **by this author.**

## Five Senses

In our *now*, we have the flesh. We have our five senses. We have our symptoms, we have our issues, and our problems. We have all the stuff that we can see because mostly man is just looking around and *seeing*. We have all of those problems that we can sense-, that's our *now*.

But God's now has the resolution of those problems. God's **NOW** says we are healed. God's NOW says that debt is retired. God's NOW says that your child is now off of the street. God's NOW says, you do have a new job, and yes, you have that promotion. You have a new house. You have all of the things that you need that pertain to life and godliness.

So, praying from God's NOW is really how you upgrade your life.

Instead, if we remain in our flesh, we are basically asking God to come into our natural life. In other words, to come from where He is sitting on high, sitting in our future, seeing what good things He has prepared for us and how we have already walked into those things.

Seriously? We want God to backtrack and come back to us. Why? Jesus already came and said, **Where I am you could be there also,** (John 14:3). So we want to walk very slowly, by the flesh, with all its distractions, do what we want to do, (like children), get into trouble (probably daily) and then ask God to come and rescue us every day.

Really?

We want to beckon for God, saying, *Oh, God, come here.*

It doesn't work like that. We're supposed to ascend in things of God, we're supposed to ascend in the spiritual matters, not just staying where we are, wallowing in the natural, wallowing in the flesh and crying out to God to come and save us.

Even in the natural, the person of higher degree, higher pedigree, higher position, higher honor **is honored**. God doesn't *wait* on us. God doesn't come at our beck and call, but we are seeking Him. God is royalty. He is King of kings. He deserves the honor. He deserves the praise. He deserves the worship.

Would you tell your boss at work to go get you a coffee? Okay, then.

And why is everything an emergency?

Is it because you need to Upgrade your life?

The crux of this chapter, this book even is: Why is your prayer life only up to today? Why is your prayer life only up to tonight?

*What*?

Yeah, it's probably because you need to upgrade your life. If you are only praying today about today, you need an upgrade. If you are in a crisis, or crisis after crisis and you are praying about right now all the time, you definitely need an upgrade.

## Your Prayers

Why is your prayer life only up to tomorrow or the day after tomorrow and why are you praying **emergency** prayers?

God is already in our tomorrow's. He's already in your tomorrow, *every* tomorrow, all of your tomorrow's. Your whole life, even your eternity, your afterlife. God is in all of that. We don't have to doubt that God is already in our tomorrow.

Fear not. God is already there.
(Luke 12:22-31)

God is already there. **So, if God is already in your tomorrow, and you desire to be, and you're trying to be in the presence**

**of God, then *why aren't you also already in your tomorrow*, too?**

Let's say you are worshipping, and you are successful in pressing forward into the presence of God. If you are in God's presence, that means you're also in your *tomorrow.* Then, why are you talking to God today about today? Because that's yesterday to God; He's already in your tomorrow.

In God's presence, why aren't we talking to God about and praying about the *day* that God is in? **Getting into God's presence and talking to God about our life, by faith is how we upgrade our life.** We upgrade our prayer life. If we have only set the next hour or two, day--, 24 hours in agreement with God, then anything is loosed to happen in your life in the next time period after that. The *anything's* of our life, things that have not been set in order, and the randomness that many embrace and call *going with the flow*, or *living in the moment*-- are what can throw us into survival mode.

We must ask ourselves, why is our prayer life only up to today, tonight, tomorrow, or the day after tomorrow?

# Vision

Vision is why we have mission statements, vision statements, mottoes, creeds. This is why we seek out our spiritual purpose. It's to get us out of just **today--,** out of being just now minded and near-sighted.

Man is a complex organism. He is a spiritual being having an earthly experience. So, we should be thinking *spiritually*. We should be thinking eternally, not just temporally, not just about the here and now, and only what we can see and taste and smell and feel.

Yes, the present is a gift. Thank You, Jesus. But we should also be looking *forward*.

Visions and mission statements propel us into our future. Purpose propels us into our future and reminds us that we *have* a future. These things make us realize that our *now, our present* is a gift. However, if we think that there's only now, only *our* now, that there is no later on, or tomorrow, no next year, we may make human mistakes, thinking of only now, instead of thinking also of our future. Here are some common erroneous thoughts:

- **It really doesn't matter**. I might as well go ahead and do this, or
- **We only live once**. Or,
- **I should go for this because there's only *now*.**

But that is not true. These are devilish temptations.

Is our prayer life so limited because do we not think that we have anything to talk to God about?

Yeah, we may think we only have to talk to God about the day--, *this* day, the day that <u>we</u> <u>**see**</u>. So we wake up in the morning, *see* what our day looks like *to us*, with our eyes of flesh, and then tell God about it like He doesn't know anything about it.

We tell God the things that we think we need regarding that day. When God already knows all of it. He knows more about it, because He is Omniscient; He knows everything. He knew it before you or it were ever formed, because He made the day, and you.

Duh--, looking at the day and seeing what we need to do *that* day is what we do with fellow humans. The morning meeting, the AM huddle. We talk about this right now stuff, and that's all. Of course, humans are finite, limited, flesh creatures. There's not a lot of use in giving a long-range plan for the entire year all at once to most humans. They will most likely forget if they even listen at all.

The sky is lowering, there will be rain—humans may share the weather report for that day or the next few days. The report of what was going on that would most likely affect their **business and MONEY** for the day, giving no concern to the *spiritual* climate of that same time period. They stopped looking, noticing, discerning once they had assessed the MONEY climate for the day.

That's right up there with checking to see if he or she is good looking to decide if you want to date or marry someone then looking no further or deeper. In so many cases like that, a man or a woman has married their own enemy. They have married the types that God would not have them to marry – people who worship at *strange altars*.

God doesn't overload us with information – He knows how much we can or will retain. Just because humans are finite beings, we can't treat God as if He is finite; He is infinite, in being, in Wisdom in capacity.

Unsaved, unregenerated man is the one who has the tendency to forget with limited brain capacity. The Holy Spirit revealed to me decades ago that the saved, Spirit-filled man uses 100 percent of his brain while the unregenerated man is muddling by on 10%.

So we wake up in the morning, assess the day and then foolishly want to go by the flesh and give God commands on what to do regarding *our* flesh, from our flesh. No, that is not pleasing to God and it's also not faith.

If you recall, successful people in the Bible, for instance, looked far ahead of the here and now. God gave Abraham the promise of Isaac 24 years before it happened, and Abraham was already old when he got the plan from God.

Don't get me wrong, yeah, there are times that you may **have** to talk to God about today. Emergency situations may take people by surprise.

Emergency situations may have taken any of us by surprise at any time. Could be, because maybe we weren't doing the stuff we're supposed to do in the natural, like, oh, I don't know--, opening your mail, reading it. I don't know--, answering the phone. Maybe, I don't know, going to work. Putting gas in your car? Eating right. Exercising.

Of course, there may be some surprises, sometimes that are no fault of your own. Ancestral, foundational ambushes. Witchcraft delays and stagnation? Keep reading, we'll get to that.

But it could be that we may be getting surprised because there are things that we may not be doing in the **spiritual** realm. Are we doing spiritual disciplines such as *watching and praying?* Hopefully we are not making spiritual mistakes such as not having a pastor and having no spiritual or prayer covering. Or stuff like not being connected to the Body of Christ to avail ourselves of intercessors and prophets and seers and visionaries and counselors and to develop our own spiritual gifts can lead to spiritual disaster. Those things are our fault.

If we're just continually living in emergency situations every day--. Why? Are we a cop? A paramedic? A firefighter, military person? An ER doc? A nurse? A trauma surgeon? Are we any of those things? Are we those essential workers? You know those essential workers are there for us to help people like us handle emergencies, not for themselves. The people in those professions snatch people out of life and death situations, they save lives, taking people out of physical survival mode day and night. So, if we're not working in any of those professions, we shouldn't be inundated with emergencies. We shouldn't be crying out to God with emergencies all the time.

Constant emergencies define survival mode.

Plan much? Of course, we plan. We plan things all the time. Some people have planned what they're going to wear for the next month. Some people are already planning and praying for their sports team to win next week, maybe even to win the playoffs. We have menu planners, people who know what their families are going to eat for the next few weeks or so. Daily bread, yeah, but not *just* daily bread.

# Survival Mode is for Babies

Survival Mode is for babies, Survival mode is for nomads, and the unsaved. Civilized people don't live in survival mode. Survival mode is either forced by violence, like wars, by generational curses, or, if by choice, by our own negligence, and it shows an unprosperous soul.

**Symptoms of survival mode match witchcraft attack.** A witchcraft attack can drive a person into survival mode, or *feeling* as if they are in survival mode. *(More on this later.)*

So why aren't we talking to God more? Why aren't we talking to God and taking our relationship with God more seriously and less for granted? Are we like a bad friend who doesn't call or text unless they want something? We say we love God; we say He's, our friend.

Seriously, if we were to spend time with God, that is, just watch and pray for one hour, we won't run out of stuff to talk to God about, will we? Well, if we only talk to Him about what we see with our natural senses, then maybe, surely, we will.

Most people who go to God to ask Him for stuff aren't in a conversation or a relationship with God, they are just **placing their order** and not taking time to listen to God.

It's God, not Alexa.

When we start praying for future things and we start putting our future in order, getting more into the NOW where God is, praying regarding the future. And that's when we are moving in faith. That's when we are praying regarding the future, praying for your future, praying into the **NOW** where God is way ahead of what we see with our natural eyes.

If we were farmers, wouldn't we be praying for the harvest when the seed is planted? We wouldn't just pray, *"Well, Lord, I hope it rains tomorrow,"* and that's all you think about that seed you just planted. Not if you're a real farmer.

No, you'd be planning nine or ten months in advance as to how long it's gonna take for this seed to harvest maybe two or three years if it's like a fruit tree, for instance.

I salute real visionaries, people with real faith. Today, **I salute you for putting a prayer covering over your whole life.** There's nothing wrong with doing that. A prayer covering over your whole future, over your purpose, over your reason for being here, even over your future generations is faith. Because without faith, it is impossible to please God.

Survival Mode is for babies and for baby Christians.

More on seeds & harvests in the series, **The Fold** by this author.

## Looking Out

God sits high in the spiritual realm but looks low; we should be spiritual but not look down *on* people but at our own situations. We know that God knows our tomorrow's and our next weeks. We know too, that we need to pray so Heaven and Earth can agree, in order to make some things happen that need to happen in our lives. We have to do that.

One of the ways we do that is in Matthew 16:19. One of the keys to the Kingdom is binding and *loosing*. This is spiritual warfare, yet another kind of prayer. Every prayer is not petition. Declaring and decreeing, where we make Heaven and Earth agree, is a type of prayer.

We must learn all the types of prayer, there's a prayer of supplication, where we worship and honor God for His Majesty, for who He is, and we respectfully, with adoration, ask Him for things. Yes, that is a petition prayer.

There's intercessory prayer. When we pray for others, or when others pray in our stead, when we are not in the same place together when the prayer is going forth.

There's a prayer of Thanksgiving where we are thankful for the things God has already done for us in the present, in the past, and we can even go into God's *NOW* and thank Him in the future for the things that He's doing for us in our now and in our future. Praying in general and this method in prayer is an upgrade to your life.

There's a prayer of praise, a prayer of repentance which we must do to be saved, believing that God sent His Son to save us.

There's a corporate prayer, a prayer for agreement, a listening prayer which is more like a dialogue, talking with God and listening for guidance from God.

Continual prayer, perpetual, prevailing prayer, is prayer, 24/7. There are breath prayers where you just say, *Thank You Jesus*.

So, we say what God says. We speak the Word of God. We do things just like He did. If we do that we will find our lives much more successful.

## Do What God Does

Back in the Garden of Eden, we can follow God's lead and do what He did in the Garden. God called for the Light when there was darkness over the face of the deep.

You call for the light in your life over your situation, and then you rightly divide the light from the darkness. Do exactly what God does.

Divide the powers, the waters from above, from the waters below, and we see what is godly and what is not godly.

Then we plant something in the Earth such as grasses and trees, yeah, in the garden. But we plant ideas, we plant thoughts, we plant purpose. We plant the Word, and we watch it grow. We command the things we plant to be fruitful and to multiply, as God has instructed.

We take Dominion, and we should; we receive the Lord's blessings, and then we rest in Him.

Later on, God created Adam. When you get married, maybe you'll create some people, too. Don't rush it.

## What Do We Pray?

So, we do the Word, we speak the Word. We do what God says. Well, you may be saying, *What do I pray for again now? What do I pray for next week and next month and then the future?*

This is why you need a heavenly language, because sometimes we don't know what to pray for like we ought. Sometimes we need to pray things that confound the enemy, so the enemy doesn't get into what we're doing and mess it up.

We pray for the things that God has prepared for us. We pray the Scriptures, we pray the Word, we pray what we know. We pray what the pastor said we should pray for.

We pray what the Prophet has spoken to us; we pray the prophetic word over our lives. We pray what we expect in God, and we pray by faith.

We pray for our needs; My God shall supply all your needs according to His riches in Glory.

We pray our dreams. Yes. We pray our dreams to cancel the demonic ones and accept the dreams from God inspired by the Holy Spirit. We pray for the Holy Spirit to bring our dreams to our remembrance and give us proper Christian interpretation so we will know how further to pray and direct our lives. Dreams are a spiritual key to our natural life.

Dreams from God are all through the Bible, but I don't know many people who teach it. I know of one "pastor" who laughs at people's dreams. Nothing scriptural about that. God spoke to people through dreams all through the Bible. God is not mocked.

We pray the vision and the mission statement of our lives, and our family's lives. Pray the vision of our bloodline. Do you know what that even is? Does your family, have a mission statement? Does it have a vision? If not, ask God. Ask God, what is the purpose of our family on Earth? What are we here to do, to learn, to go through? Who are we here to bless? What is our part in Your divine plan?

Ever wonder?

Then ask God.

Pray for things that are lovely and have good report and have virtue. Pray and ask God to perfect the matters that concern you, (Psalm 139). Pray for Wisdom and understanding. Pray to grow in Grace. Pray to grow in Truth and Knowledge and in the Word. Pray the Word of God. Pray to grow in spiritual matters. Pray for the Fruit of the Spirit. Pray for more Fruit and Fruit that remains. Pray to be more Christ-like. Pray that God has an expected end for you, your life, your family, and your bloodline, (Jeremiah 29:11).

Pray to be kept in perfect health. Pray for healing and long-life purpose, satisfaction, fulfillment, good success. Pray for peace.

Pray for your works and your good works in the Earth.

You do need a heavenly language. Pray to know what that is and to receive the Holy Spirit after Salvation.

Pray *from* your future. Pray to spend time with God to hear His voice and obey His direction.

Pray to have vision. Pray about your spiritual gifts.

Speak those things that be not just like God did.

When you have more faith, pray in God's **NOW** because you know **it's already finished** where God is. You are already saved. You are already Spirit-filled, you are already healed, you are already whole, you are already prosperous. In God, you are already everything that God says you are.

But sometimes we don't know what to pray for like we ought so this is why you need a heavenly language, to upgrade your life confound the enemy and also speak directly to God using that language.

**Pray and <u>say</u>.**

## Is It Real?

Survival Mode is a supposed to be a short-term event in your life, as when people may feel as though they are under attack or overly stressed. When under attack or feeling as if you are under attack, the body elicits a response called the Fight or Flight, and in some cases a *Freeze* Response.

This response is triggered in people in order to save their life--, either to help them overtake the enemy or to get away from the enemy. In some cases, a human may freeze and not know what to do. Survival mode is triggered by a trauma, such as a severe loss or perceived big changes in life. These could be real big changes, but it could just be *perceived* changes.

All of this is dependent upon our filters, our thought process, our soul prosperity, how we see things, how we process things, how we feel things, how we function in our lives.

So big and or small changes impact people differently. It depends, as I said, on who you are, what you've been through, your upbringing and what world you were born into.

For instance, some people are born into a world of stress and chronic stress and danger. Some are born into a house of danger. Some were born into a family that is either very stressful or could be dangerous.

Or you could live in a place where you felt as though you were in eminent danger. In these situations, the feelings of survival mode are passed down generationally to children. It could be that the children *never* experience any danger at all, but the parents may be so traumatized themselves that their fears, worries, and their concerns are passed on to their children in the name of love.

Real or perceived, it is transferred to the children as ***real***.

For instance an unhealed but traumatized adult may want to protect their child at all cost from going through what they went through as a child. But their child is not even IN the situation the parent was in. We see this in the overprotective, or hovering, sometimes, controlling parent. Often, we see this as just plain weird.

# Real Survival Mode

This book discusses real survival mode. Most often it is an acute thing, a sudden thing, but sometimes it could be chronic, as in families. But it is survival mode where you *feel* that the risk is real, the danger is real to life and survival. You feel there is a risk of bodily harm, either to yourself or to someone that you have care of, or sometimes to something that you have care or need of, like your car or your house--, your dog.

Ask yourself before we begin and before you process this information, what is your situation? Are you really in danger, or do you just *think* you're in danger or at risk? Are you really stressed, or do you just *think* you are? Are you really in survival mode or do you just *think* you are just because things aren't going your way?

You are not really in survival mode if you don't have a new car, but your neighbor does. I'm not talking about that; being a desperate housewife is not real survival mode. I'm not talking about comparing yourself to others and what others have. I'm not talking about being in competition with other people. The risk here is that survival mode can lead you into comparison-itis where you are comparing yourself to others, needlessly so.

We are talking about real survival mode, most likely. It's sudden, possibly chronic, but there's a **real** danger to life or to bodily harm or to losing something or someone that you really need for life. Something or someone that you have charge over such as children or parents relatives may be in jeopardy.

Check yourself to see if you're really in survival mode. You might be if you have any of these markers:

1. It does take *all that* to make it through the day.

2. You can feel overwhelmed, as though you can only deal with today, maybe the next 24 hours, nothing more.

3. Everything feels urgent. Everything *is* urgent. You're in crisis mode.

4. You are reacting, not responding.

5. There's one fire and then the next.

6. You're rushing, rushing, rushing everywhere, but you don't feel like you're getting anywhere.

7. Nobody's listening to you. Nobody can hear what you need them to hear to help you. But no one is helping you. No one *can* help you. You feel like you've got to do it all yourself.

9. Folks are getting in your way. They need to get out of your way so you can handle this.

10. You might go off on somebody, you might snap on somebody, and

11. You don't eat or sleep properly.

That's only the beginning. There may be more. Next, we will look into the somatic (bodily) effects of survival mode. This is where the rubber really meets the road.

## What Stress Feels Like

In times of crisis, we may enter into survival mode. There, our normal, thinking, rational, processing brain, which solves problems and organizes our lives and regulates our emotions, does our critical thinking, helps us to make logical decisions IT KIND OF GOES retrograde because with stress, another part of our nervous system takes over.

The sympathetic nervous system takes over and ushers in a fight or flight, or freeze response that mentioned earlier, and it technically hijacks the body and the brain.

Then a series of stress hormones are released into the body. Adrenaline, norepinephrine, and cortisol are stress hormones. Caution: Do not make long-term decisions when your rational mind is hijacked or retrograde, when your emotional mind has taken over, do not make long term or serious decisions like getting married, changing jobs, moving, divorcing, having children.

When the brain is in survival mode, it thinks it is in SAFE MODE, as when your computer crashes but miraculously brings itself back up. It may or may not know how to do the basics, but it *thinks* it does. Survival mode is NOT a safe mode, but your body thinks it is handling things. And maybe it is handling things as well as they can be handled. Right now.

In survival mode the body releases adrenaline and cortisol and epinephrine and norepinephrine while in a state of acute stress and is really barely hanging on.

Survival mode, this can lead to mental, emotional, and body fatigue. You are worn out emotionally and mentally, but at the same time your emotions are on edge. You're upset. You could be angry; you could be lashing out at people--, in drama mode, crying.

Over a longer term, you may gain weight or lose weight. Usually whichever one you don't want, that's what you'll get.

Your brain is fuzzy. Your memory is off. You can't figure out what to do next— possibly due to a lack of sleep. Not necessarily though, **evil arrows** could have been fired at your head or your brain.

I'll stop here and describe what an evil arrow is. It is a spiritual weapon that can wound, damage, trouble, afflict, or even kill a person. They are from the powers of darkness, and they are invisible. You don't believe in that? It's still real, whether you believe it or not. There are two types of evil arrows, one of affliction and one of death. Stay prayed up, people you don't even know may hate you and send evil arrows. Sometimes as vacuously as, saying, or muttering, *"I wish she would..."* That's a blind curse. That's an evil arrow.

Then there are the types who do evil for a living. You don't want to be a candidate for either. If an arrow doesn't take a person out, it will afflict them and send them into survival mode, which torments and diminishes their successes, and the quality of their life.

In chronic survival mode you may be entering into metabolic syndrome, which is dangerous because it may lead to heart disease and possibly type 2 diabetes. You may experience high blood pressure, high cholesterol, and possibly autoimmune disorders.

These are real things that happen. Whether you are really in acute stress and survival mode or whether you just *think* you are. Seriously, your body, your mind may not know the difference.

If you perceive that you're in stress, then you *<u>are</u>* in stress and your body will give you that reaction. If your mind can believe an evil thing, without spiritual intervention you may do the rest of the damage to yourself, yourself.

Let's recap the affects of being in stress:

The mind may lose concentration or lose some part of the memory, so you don't want to really have to be making long term decisions while you're in this state of mind, in a state of survival mode. However, you must make immediate decisions, else how will you get OUT of survival mode?

Let's say you get a severe, stabbing stomach pain, it is out of the blue, your rational mind is so overrun and now in retrograde. You are thinking about what happened to your grandma and all the worst things that could have caused this, so you can't even THINK that you have ginger drops at your house and that you use a few of them to remedy this condition. So, you suffer. And worry. And imagine scenarios. Then you suffer some more.

In your gut, in your GI tract, you may end up with some Pepto Bismol moments like nausea, heartburn, upset stomach, diarrhea.

Because the blood goes away from the digestive tract into the muscles, so you can either get away as in a flight response, or overtake your real opponent or *imagined* opponent, as in a fight response. The decrease of blood to your GI system may lead to indigestion eventually, if it lasts a long time. Eventually, malnutrition could result, where you can't uptake your vitamins and your nutrients properly may result.

Effects of feelings of survival mode on the heart are chronic stress which may lead to heart disease, high blood pressure as we discussed, peripheral vascular disease, heart failure, heart attack, stroke, especially if your family line is already susceptible to any of these disorders.

Your immune system is suppressed by survival mode and that makes you at a greater risk of contracting even small diseases, maybe even bigger things, but we'll say colds, flu, that sort of thing, while cuts and scrapes and things may take longer to heal because your immune system is suppressed.

All in all, in survival mode you may suffer anxiety, depression, high blood pressure, weight changes, sleep disorders, nightmares, drug or alcohol addiction as you try to fix it yourself, other addictions such as sex or gambling, fertility issues, or other physical ailments.

Teeth grinding? Yeah, that's a real thing. Acne, hives, severe PMS, carb and sugar cravings, which lead to worse problems because you're looking for *comfort food.* Know that food is also a drug. You may suffer migraines, canker sores, sores, hair loss, wrinkles, and any and all of this stuff could lead to **more stress**. It becomes a vicious cycle.

The average person who's in survival mode is probably thinking in their mind, how can I get out of this? How? What can I do to get out of this? So that puts you in flesh mode, which is also a selfish mode.

So, survival mode makes you very selfish because you're thinking about your survival and you're thinking, *Why me?* Your go-to behavior is to do everything you know to do to save your life. I think this is only natural.

In survival mode you might be thinking, *I don't have enough, What about me? I need this, I need that. I need everything.* Survival mode, long term, could make a person into a hoarder.

Survival mode is fear mode. You fear for your safety. You may fear for your actual life, or for the safety or the life of people that you have charge over. You could be worried about the status of your pet, your house, your car, your relatives, your children.

But God has not given us the *spirit of fear*, but of love power and a sound mind. Therefore, we're supposed to do like Jesus would do and to embrace the sound mind so we can **logically** get ourselves through this and *spiritually* the Lord will get us through and out of survival mode into the mode of soul prosperity and where we're supposed to be in God as we get an **Upgrade** out of survival mode.

Fear will put you into flight or a fight mentality. As I said, if it comes upon you, survival mode is supposed to be a short-lived thing, especially in a civilized society.

Unless you're in a war--, then that's another whole conversation.

## Flesh Mode

How do we get out of survival mode?

The first thing you should do is look at the problem and try to embrace the lesson. Sometimes the lesson is to teach you something about yourself, and it might just be that you are to do the opposite of what you would normally do.

Still, pray about it. You also need to ask God and godly people about your situation. Research what would Jesus do in this situation. Crises are sometimes lessons, trials, and tests. Sometimes it's a test of how you will perform under pressure so you can learn *yourself* better.

But what would Jesus do?

What is soul prosperity? We'll get to this.

If you're not saved, you should get saved because you see the Kingdom of God enjoys peace and joy in the Holy Spirit. You want the things of God such as peace and joy? Do you want out of survival mode? Then get saved and ask for and receive the Holy Spirit because there is righteousness, peace, and joy in the Holy Ghost.

Be sure you get a spiritual covering such as a pastor. Have a prayer covering by having a real prayer life yourself. You can receive godly counseling. In prayer you can go into more prayers and fast. You may need deliverance.

Some of the problems that you or anyone might be struggling with may only come out by prayer, and fasting.

Pray first to make sure the problem is not a spiritual problem, because there is no natural cure for a spiritual problem. The symptoms of witchcraft attack by evil arrows will usually yield nothing at the medical doctor's office, other than a roll of the eyes because they can't find anything wrong with you.

But you may choose to do the natural things first, obeying natural laws. Maybe the problem you're in is because you broke the natural laws. You obey civil laws, don't you? You should obey spiritual laws, and you do want a prosperous soul, don't you? For soul prosperity, keep your mind stayed on God.

> Beloved I pray above all things that you prosper and be in health even as your soul prospers, (3 John 2).

Your survival issue might be financial, it might be health-related, it might be physical.

So, get yourself a spiritual life and get in the Word of God. If you can't read the Word of God, at least listen to some teaching ministry. There's an abundance of it out here. Obey spiritual laws; it will give you a mighty defense against evil arrows shot at you by people you know, as well as those coming from evil strangers.

Obey the laws of sin and death, that is as much as is in you. Don't break spiritual laws. Don't become a sinner because death is the normal sequela of sin. Obey the laws of Seedtime and Harvest. You are to become fruitful and multiply and replenish and subdue the Earth; do what God said.

Get a spiritual life. Put down the works of the flesh, and instead begin to try to operate in the Fruit of the Spirit.

## Get Out of It

What we've learned is that survival mode is a flesh mode. Put down the works of the flesh to get out of survival mode. It would be a vicious cycle to keep operating in the flesh while trying to get out of a flesh problem.

Alright, so now we set our minds in order to get out of survival mode. Ask yourself, *Do you really want to get out of survival mode?* OK, so now you do. Now you put your mind on God. God says that He'll keep you in perfect peace if you keep your mind stayed on Him. So, you think on the things of God. You think on the things that are lovely, that have virtue, that have good report that are true, and on things where there's love. Speak the Word of God out loud in prayers and whenever you can. That is *meditating* on the Word.

Being Godly doesn't mean you become a doormat. It just means you **think on better things than you're probably used to think on.** Your thought life could have actually gotten you into this problem.

Then you start **<u>doing</u>** the works of the Fruit of the Spirit. Be loving, joyful peaceful; chill out. Don't let things get you riled up. Easy to say, but it will take practice to actually do this. Be gentle, meek, and show goodness and temperance to people. Learn to respond, where you would normally react. Get your works in order. Be taught, sit at the feet of teachers and be taught, resist the devil (flesh), learn what right responses are.

Depending on what kind of household you were brought up in and what was modeled before you, this may be easy, hard, or very difficult to do. But these are the steps to getting out of survival mentality, and survival mode.

But the fruit of the Spirit is love, joy, peace, longsuffering, gentleness, goodness, faith, meekness, temperance: against such there is no law. (Galatians 5:22-23)

***Against which there is no law...*** From the above verse that means that no one can blame you for anything if you follow after the Fruit of the Spirit. Quickly, Satan is the accuser of the brethren. He stands at the throne of God day and night accusing God's people. It's a court; so if a person is being accused and a verdict is rendered against that person, based on the Law of God, and that person broke any of the Laws of God, then the devil has won. Even if the devil enticed you or tricked you into breaking the Law, it is still a win for him and a defeat for you.

If the devil has won, then torment, damage, theft, robbery, affliction, even death, through a satanic evil arrow becomes a legal thing for the devil to do to the person who had a judgment passed against him. Whether this person knew there was a court case against him in Heaven, or not.

Therefore, dear reader, if you are operating in the Fruit of the Spirit, versus the works of the flesh, the devil cannot get a verdict against you and cannot afflict you or interfere in your life by means of witchcraft, and you will go unmolested by the devil and his evil agents in the Earth.

As Jesus said, He has nothing in Me, Jesus meant the devil had nothing on Him, and therefore had no grounds to trouble Him, and no way to entrap Him. We all should endeavor to be like Jesus, else we will need to fight evil arrows over and again until we defeat them and live upright before the Lord.

> Hereafter I will not talk much with you: for the prince of this world cometh, and hath nothing in me. (John 14:30)

Do not feel condemned, we all have sinned and come short of the Glory of God. And sometimes the evil that is coming against you is *ancestral* and it's not even your fault. But if you are afflicted, it is your problem.

And, if you are aware of it, then you must do something about it, spiritually, or it will jump you into survival mode and hinder or ruin your life.

When you feel that you are really in survival mode, look at what other people in Scripture did in stressful situations.

Daniel and his three friends were in the fiery furnace. What did they do?

**They trusted God**.

Paul and Silas were in jail at midnight. What did they do?

**They praised their way out**; they were praising God. Hallelujah.

What did Jesus do?

Jesus was going to the Cross, the epitome of stressful situations. Jesus ended up **giving in to the will of God**. He says, *Not my will, but thine*. Don't fight against God.

So, these are things you can do. Trust God, praise God, give in to the will of God because God has the best things for your life.

He's already planned the best for your life. He's not trying to do you any harm. His plans are of peace and plans of an expected and a prosperous end.

Disobeying God is what may have gotten you, or any of us into the stressful situation in the first place.

> Now the works of the flesh are manifest, which are these; Adultery, fornication, uncleanness, lasciviousness,
>
> Idolatry, witchcraft, hatred, variance, emulations, wrath, strife, seditions, heresies,
>
> Envyings, murders, drunkenness, revellings, and such like: of the which I tell you before, as I have also told you in time past, that they which do such things shall not inherit the kingdom of God. (Galatians 5:19-21)

I think of Jonah and the whale. Jonah was supposed to go someplace. He did the **opposite** of what God said, and he got swallowed up by a whale. If God already told you **not** to do a thing, not to connect with certain folks, but you did it anyway, the first thing you need to do is repent.

Another thing you can do to get out of survival mode, and stay out of it is to make sure you are connected properly with other believers. Warning: Not people who *say* they are believers, not people who just *look* like they are believers, but real believers. You have to discern every *spirit* and ASK GOD. See, you've got to always be in prayer.

It's better to have a neighbor close by than a brother far off. The Scripture tells us that two is better than one. Maybe he's talking about marriage, but two friends are better than just one person standing alone. The Word also says that a threefold cord is not easily broken, so you get the Holy Spirit in there, and that friendship won't be easily broken.

If you reject the works of the flesh, including sexual immorality, impurity, sensuality, idolatry, sorcery, enmity, strife, jealousy, fits of anger, rivalries, dissensions, divisions, envy, orgies, drunkenness, and things like that, (Galatians 5:19-21). If you reject that, then you will be working in the Fruit of the Spirit.

If you will <u>not</u> give into the flesh, then people will come and help you, when they see you're not an awful person that they don't want to be around. Like a person who is moving in pride, for instance, people will come and help you if you drop the pride. Get some humility. People are pretty decent in this Earth, still.

So instead of flesh works do spiritual works and the Fruit of the Spirit is love, joy, peace, forbearance, kindness, goodness, faithfulness. Gentleness and self-control against which there is no law, (Galatians 5:22,23).

Recapping: Set your mind in order. Set your works in order. Set your life in order, and this includes your money.

# A Test Deposit

You might already know this, but God will send a test deposit into your bank account, or into the account of your life. God will send a test of deposit into your *account* and what does God want you to do with that? Pay close attention to this, **especially if your survival problem is financial.** Maybe you are in survival mode, because of money.

God sends this test deposit into your account. He wants you to confirm that you are a child of God and that you've received it. That test deposit means that in response, you're going to send something *back* to God to prove that yes, you are a child of God and you received what He gave you. What you sent back to God is the **tithe**.

Test deposits prove that it's definitely your account and it also connects you to the account that sent the initial deposit. This is what you need for your life, financially speaking.

Survival mode can make you ungrateful, selfish and like a hoarder, and it makes you not want to tithe. Remember sometimes to get out of survival mode you've got to do the *exact opposite* of the thing that you did, which is what got you into trouble in the first place.

Not tithing could show that you are ungrateful. Not giving offerings shows that you are ungrateful, disobedient, and have no faith. It could be an indication that you have a money stronghold. You could have an ancestral altar holding you back from tithing or giving in general. BUT it is keeping you in captivity--, the captivity of survival mode.

In order to get out of survival mode now, **pray and say.**

## Chill Out

There are other neurotransmitters in your body besides the stress hormones. Oxytocin, dopamine, and serotonin are released into the body to **improve** your health, to improve your sleep, to help your immune system, and to help your digestion. These are activated, yes, when you are calm, when you are peaceful, when you meditate, and **pray.**

Yes. When you meditate and pray, there are *physiological* changes in your body that God has established to heal you, help you, bless you, and **bring you out of survival mode.**

Survival mode would lead you to either attack somebody or to run away, rather than talk to people. Talking to folks is civilized, it is soul prosperity. Just have a conversation, have a dialogue, look at the problem straight on and handle it.

Sometimes you need to do the *opposite* of what stress tells you to do. Use your words; a prospered soul will use their words.

Meditate on the Word and pray. So here are things you do, and I got this out of the Good Book, right out of the Bible. Overarching answers to what the problem could be to help you out of survival mode, to help any of us out of survival mode are:

1. **Find Jesus**. Reach out to Jesus like the woman with the issue of blood, touch the hem of His garment.
2. **Pray the prayer faith**. If you can't pray for yourself, have somebody to pray for you. Call for the elders of the church; they will pray for you. The intercessors, the prayer warriors will pray for you.
3. **Ask God**. Seek, Knock. Ask. You will get answers.

4. **Fill other people up** with what God has given you. If you're saved and Spirit-filled, you have an anointing. Use your gifts. Use your anointing. Cheerful giving makes you cheerful and that releases the good hormones in your body.

Remember, survival mode makes you selfish, so do the **opposite**. To get out of survival mode, use your gifts for others.

5. **Do what the Prophet says**. Obey the Prophet and you will get the prophet's reward.
6. **Bless the Prophet** or bless the man of God the woman of God.
7. **Find a kinsman Redeemer**. Ruth had found Boaz, rather Boaz found Ruth a kinsman Redeemer.

Jesus is our Redeemer. We don't need to find a kinsman Redeemer; I'm **not** telling you to get a sugar daddy or sugar Mama. I'm not recommending any of that. Find the kinsman Redeemer; Jesus is our Redeemer.

**8. Get to where the anointing or the power of God is.**

When God is stirring the water, the man at Bethesda said he didn't have anybody to put him in the water, so he wasn't rightly *connected* with people. Granted, he didn't have any people to help him get in that water. But when God is stirring the water, when the anointing is stirred, where the power and the anointing of God is, is where you need to be in order to receive healing or blessing or reversal of whatever the curse or the problem is in your life that's causing the survival mentality, or survival mode.

9. **Rise up and walk**. This is especially for people who would normally hide or retreat under stress. **Do the opposite**. Be strong. In faith, rise up and walk.
10. **Wrestle with the Angel of God**. Jacob did this.

Jacob said to the Angel of God, *"I'm not going to let go until you bless me."* So, you stay in there. You stay in warfare, you stay in the Word, you stay in prayer, and you ask God.

Let the Lord know that you can't let go until He blesses you. Declare it, *Lord, until this Angel blesses me, I won't let go.*

11. **Dig some wells**. In other words, do some work.

Abraham dug wells. They got covered over by the jealous Philistines. His son Isaac re-dug the wells. You say sometimes stress and survival mode is caused by a lack of feelings of success. So, you work until you *feel* successful and then be thankful.

12. **Believe in God** and
13. **Praise**

Remember, Paul and Silas got out of jail by praising. They got out of a very real survival mode, out of stress, out of prison by praising God, loudly at midnight.

Of course, you want to prosper your soul. An unprospered soul is easily triggered. You don't want to be triggered all the time. But until you are, know you're your triggers are and protect yourself against them. Set boundaries. Then insist on your boundaries. Don't let people run all over you.

Eat right. Change your diet because your survival mode, your stress mode could be caused by caffeine and other stimulants. You could be just agitated because of that.

You could be agitated by high blood pressure, maybe you need to get a checkup. You could be agitated because your blood sugar is not balanced. Maybe you also need to get a checkup and change your diet. OK, change your diet. We talked about that.

Now you might want to go alkaline because you may be filled with inflammation because your body is too acidic. By changing your diet, you are changing your whole system.

Drink plenty of water. Drink good water. I recommend alkaline water with a pH of 9 to 10, but some say it doesn't matter. There's regular water, which is fine if it has a pH of about 7 but check your water to make sure the water that you're drinking does not have a pH of *less* than 7 because that is acidic.

Sport drinks, energy drinks and sodas have a pH in the 2.0 to 3.0 range. They will send your body into inflammation so quickly.

**Battery acid has a pH of 1.** This should help you decide on the best beverage for you.

Inflammation is the start of almost every disease in humans; inflammation and disease can send you into survival mode.

Remember to meditate and pray and get some sleep, get some rest, go sleep.

Decrease your own stress and you can live better and longer, and you can do the purpose that you were sent here to do. You can do what you're supposed to do.

You may ask yourself again, what is the cause of my stress? Is it my diet? Is it a stressful relationship? Is it jacked up finances? Is it a stressful job? What is it?

Then you will pray, and you will take positive steps to remedy the situation and not just react and stress yourself out even more.

Get rid of whatever is the cause. Ask yourself, is there really an external cause that's causing me to be this, or is it *internal*? Is it something that I'm eating or drinking? Something I'm thinking about--, over thinking, worrying about? Something I'm watching on TV? Am I watching too many horror movies and it's agitating me? Ask yourself that.

Is it violent video games? Remember neither your brain nor your body knows the difference between real and not real.

Ask yourself, is it your over-the-top response to normal stimuli? Maybe you're over emotional. You need to ask yourself these questions; learn to prosper in your soul, which is your will, your intellect, and your emotions.

The Word of God is the key to soul prosperity.

# Are You Being Manipulated?

Perhaps there are no negative stimuli leading to your feelings of stress and being in survival mode.

Perhaps, you are being *manipulated*. Maybe there's gaslighting going on in your life, or someone's trying to control or dominate you, or maybe there's a negative *spiritual* manipulation. We've mentioned evil arrows earlier and the effects of witchcraft attack are exactly like survival mode.

To walk out of survival mode we've talked about what has to be done. Even though you may be having survival symptoms don't report those; report only what God says. Agree with God in your words and thoughts.

Do what God would do. Take your position of dominion, because we are called to be in Dominion, we are created a little lower than the angels, says the Psalmist. We are then to receive of the Lord's blessings.

So repent if you haven't. Pray with intention, pray right now, If you're in survival mode, pray about that in warfare prayers. But after you're out of survival upgrade your life. Upgrade your prayer life.

Think ahead. Think of what God has already said, what the pastor has said, what the Prophet has said regarding who you are, what you already have, how you've already transcended this part. Just like God transcends space and time--, past today, past next weekend, using your words in prayers, and your faith, you can have it your way when you pray and **say**.

Use your words; pray the Word and let God light your path and put a lamp unto your feet. God says He'll make the crooked ways straight. He'll bring you out of the miry clay. He'll put your feet in a large and a green place.

He prepares rivers for you in a desert. You won't have to be dry and weak.

God says He will pour out a blessing that are so large there won't be room enough to receive it. He is El Shaddai. He is the God of more than enough.

God will open the floodgates of Heaven and the windows of Heaven for you. God will open doors that no man can shut. God will close doors that no man can open.

God will bring you to the prosperous end that He says He has for you.

**AMEN.**

***Dear Reader:***

Thank you for acquiring and reading this book. I pray it makes your life better. Survival mode is not for humans, may the Lord deliver you quickly.

*Blessings,*

*Dr. Marlene Miles*

There are three books in this Survival Mode series.

**Upgrade: How to Get Out of Survival Mode**

https://a.co/d/5SZEkcd

**Toxic Souls**

https://a.co/d/hU1z576

**Legacy**

https://a.co/d/dDhmoU1

Christian books by this author:

AK: Adventures of the Agape Kid

AMONG SOME THIEVES

As My Soul Prospers

Behave

Churchzilla: The Wanna-Be Bride of Christ

The Coco-So-So Correct Show

Demons Hate Questions

Do Not Orphan Your Seed

Do Not Work for Money

Don't Refuse Me Lord

The FAT Demons

got Money?

Let Me Have a Dollar's Worth

Living for the NOW of God

Lord, Help My Debt

Lose My Location

Made Perfect In Love

The Man Safari *(Really, I'm Just Looking)*

Marriage Ed., *Rules of Engagement & Marriage*

The Motherboard: *Key to Soul Prosperity*

*My Life As A Slave*

Name Your Seed

Plantation Souls

The Poor Attitudes of Money

Power Money: Nine Times the Tithe

The Power of Wealth

Seasons of Grief

Seasons of War

SOULS in Captivity

Soul Prosperity: Your Health & Your Wealth

The *spirit* of Poverty

The Throne of Grace, *Courtroom Prayers*

**Time Is of the Essence**

**Triangular Powers (4 book series)**

    Powers Above

    Sun Block

    Do Not Swear By the Moon

    Star Struck

**Upgrade Series**

    How To Get Out of Survival Mode

    Toxic Souls

    Legacy

**Warfare Prayer Against Poverty**

**When the Devourer is Rebuked**

**The Wilderness Romance (3 book series)**

    The Social Wilderness

    The Sexual Wilderness

    The Spiritual Wilderness

**Other Journals & Devotionals by this author:**

*The Cool of the Day – Journal* for times spent with God

**got HEALING? Verses for Life**

**got HOPE? Verses for Life**

**got WISDOM? Verses for Life**

**got GRACE? Verses for Life**

**got JOY? Verses for Life**

**got PEACE? Verses for Life**

**got LOVE? Verses for Life**

**He Hears Us, Prayer Journal** *in 4 different colors*

*I Have A Star*, **Dream Journal** *in styles for kids, teen, young adult and up.*

*I Have A Star*, **Guided Prayer Journal,** *2 styles: Boy or Girl*

***J'ai une Etoile, Journal des Reves***

**Let Her Dream, Dream Journal** *in multiple colors*

**Men Shall Dream, Dream Journal,** *(blue or black)*

*My Favorite Prayers (in 4 styles)*

*My Sowing Journal (in three different colors)*

*Tengo una Estrella, Diario de Sueños*

Wise Counsel Journal

## Illustrated children's books by this author:

*Big Dog (8-book series)*

*Do Not Say That to Me*

*Every Apple*

*Fluff the Clouds*

*I Love You All Over the World*

*Imma Dance*

*The Jump Rope*

*Kiss the Sun*

*The Masked Man*

*Not During a Pandemic*

*Push the Wind*

*Tangled Taffy*

*What If?*

*Wiggle, Wiggle; Giggle, Giggle*

*Worry About Yourself*

*You Did Not Say Goodbye to Me*

www.ingramcontent.com/pod-product-compliance
Lightning Source LLC
Chambersburg PA
CBHW070856050426
42453CB00012B/2228